Facts About Forest Fires

Sharon McConnell

The Rosen Publishing Group, Inc.
New York

Published in 2001 by The Rosen Publishing Group, Inc.
29 East 21st Street, New York, NY 10010

Copyright © 2001 by The Rosen Publishing Group, Inc.

All rights reserved. No part of this book may be reproduced in any form without permission in writing from the publisher, except by a reviewer.

Book Design: Haley Wilson

Photo Credits: Cover, pp. 1, 8 © Clyde H. Smith/FPG International; p. 4 © Image Bank; p. 6 © Wayne Aldridge/International Stock; p. 10 © Robert Graham/FPG International; p. 12 © Jeff and Alexa Henry; p. 14 © Joseph Sohm/Corbis.

ISBN: 0-8239-8138-X
6-pack ISBN: 0-8239-8540-7

Manufactured in the United States of America

Contents

What Is Fire?	5
What Does Fire Need to Burn?	7
How Does a Forest Fire Start?	9
Fighting Forest Fires	11
Smoke Jumpers	13
Forest Fire Safety	14
Glossary	15
Index	16

What Is Fire?

Fire is the light we see when something **burns**. Fire helps us in many ways. We use fire to cook our food and heat our homes. Fire can also hurt us if we are not careful with it.

We must always be careful when we are around fire.

What Does Fire Need to Burn?

Fire needs air, **fuel**, and heat to burn. Air is all around us. It is what we breathe. Fuel comes from things that burn, like wood and leaves. When air, fuel, and heat mix, a fire can start.

Fire can be dangerous if it gets out of control.

How Does a Forest Fire Start?

A forest fire is a fire that starts in the forest and burns down the trees that grow there. Some forest fires start when **lightning** hits a tree in a forest. People start most forest fires. If a campfire is left burning, a forest fire can start. The fire can spread quickly from one tree to another.

Once a fire starts, it can spread quickly.

Fighting Forest Fires

To stop a forest fire, **firefighters** clear away leaves and branches. This keeps the fire from spreading. Then the firefighters spray the fire with lots of water. This puts out the fire.

Sometimes firefighters have to work for many days or weeks to stop a forest fire.

Smoke Jumpers

Sometimes forest fires are hard to reach by truck. **Smoke jumpers** are firefighters who jump from airplanes. They land on the ground near the fire. Smoke jumpers bring tools with them to help fight the fire.

If smoke jumpers get to the fire early, they can stop it more quickly.

Forest Fire Safety

You can help keep forests safe from fire. Never play with matches or fire. If you are camping, make sure your campfire is put out before you leave the area. Remember what Smokey Bear says: "Only you can prevent forest fires."

Glossary

burn   To be on fire or set on fire.

firefighter   Someone who puts out fires.

fuel   Anything that can be burned.

lightning   A flash of light in the sky during a storm.

smoke jumper   A firefighter who reaches forest fires by jumping out of a plane.

Index

A
air, 7

B
burn(s), 5, 7, 9

C
campfire, 9, 14

F
firefighters, 11, 13
forest(s), 9, 11, 13, 14
fuel, 7

H
heat, 5, 7
hurt, 5

L
light, 5
lightning, 9

S
smoke jumpers, 13

T
tree(s), 9